Some say everything happens for a reason. I believe something much deeper than mere coincidence brought you to this book. In the following pages, I share all the tricks of the trade and give you insights into why men do the things they do to get with women. By the time you finish reading this book, you will have gained all the tools and strategies you need to make the right decisions when it comes to dating and relationships. I will also offer you many reasons why it is important to focus on what is ahead of you in your journey. You will meet some people along the way who are not meant to be in your life. You will experience obstacles that challenge your ability to make the right decisions in critical times. Those obstacles multiply the older and more successful you become.

I want to start off by apologizing to any woman I may have hurt in the past. As a young boy growing into a man, I made dumb decisions and may have hurt some women along the way. I ask you to forgive me because I am not perfect. I was once something similar to what some women would call a player, but not one of those old-school players you've heard about. They are a thing of the past. In today's society, women are surrounded by a new breed of player. This new breed, a kind of hybrid smooth-talker and pickup artist, is much wiser and sophisticated than its old-school predecessor. Welcome to the dark side of gentleman.

How do I know? Because I was once a member of this elite group, but my player ways all changed when my daughter was born. The first time I looked in her eyes I knew I had to make a change. I decided to write a letter to her containing all the advice I wanted pass on and the tactics I wanted to warn her about in case something were ever to happen to me. After much thought and consideration, I realized that many women could also benefit from this same advice, which is why I wrote this book.

Unlocking Magic is especially designed for young women going into high school and college. It ensures that parents will no longer have to worry about their daughters growing up and getting their hearts broken by selfish men. The teenage years and early twenties are when young women begin to hear the whispers of the womanizer. It is at this point that all women must read this book and arm themselves with its wisdom so that they can stay ahead of any man with ulterior motives. This book is about more than just love and relationships. It's about teaching young women to acknowledge their worth and demand that others do the same. In the age of women's empowerment and the push for gender equality, this book helps bridge the gap in dating and love. Get ready to unlock your magic.

Women, Know Your Value

You are worthy. Your value, beauty, and intelligence are far more complex than any man will ever be able to describe. You have the ability to give life. Think about that for a moment. That's why you should never let a man dictate your worth. Because it was a woman who brought him into this world.

You must realize how important and powerful your mind is. Every woman must look deep within themselves to unlock their magic and embrace their power. You were born with it. It's in your DNA. Television and social media affect the way women and girls see themselves, especially when it comes to realizing that women are men's equals, if not more. The media also try to make you think you have to look a certain way or be a certain color to be beautiful and accepted in society.

That is not true. In fact, I think a very insecure person came up with that logic. Every woman is beautiful, and often they don't even realize it. You will never be beneath anyone. I don't care what they say to you. This is why words and images should not hold any power over you unless they are positive and beneficial to you. The truth is women actually control the world. Every man who looks into a woman's eyes without malice will understand that. If he doesn't, I highly recommend you show him the exit out of your life and fast. If not, he will eventually try to control everything that you do.

You must always demand what you want. For any man that's lucky enough to talk to you, make sure to maintain strong eye contact with him. Not in a flirtatious way, but in a firm and serious way. When a woman does not make eye contact or constantly looks away in conversation, it is a sign of weakness to the man. He will instantly know whether you are attracted to him or not. Your eyes will tell a player everything he needs to know during conversation. He knows a lot of women are shy and the slight smile right before she breaks eye contact usually gives her feelings away. He may see this as an invitation to take advantage of you and add you to the long list of women he's got running. Treat every guy who approaches you as if he is a player out to conquer you.

Most guys will look at you as an object instead of the Goddess you truly are. Remember, his opinion only matters if you allow it to. You must keep an eye out for the bad in guys before you can attempt to look for the good ones. Some may call this a curse. I call it a gift once you are able to master my strategies for separating the players from the men who are genuinely looking for love.

Pretend, for a moment, that you are a basketball coach and need five players on your team. You wouldn't choose someone to be on your team who simply "says" they are good at basketball without proving themselves first. You are trying to win, right? So you go to the local gym to scout players and observe carefully before choosing your team. Your time is valuable, so you must be selective about forming your own dynasty.

The same is true of dating men and finding a partner in life. Would you rather find out a guy is no good before or after you let him into your life? A man must prove to you that he is worthy of your time and beyond. Sticking to this rule will help prevent scumbags from getting close to you.

There are a lot of women struggling right now because they trusted a man's words, looks, or charm. There are women who are raising kids by themselves because a guy told them everything they wanted to hear. The problem is he didn't keep his word. If she only knew ahead of time that he had ulterior motives and no intention of being in her future, she could have moved on and met a guy who would have treated her right.

Men will promise you the moon if that's what they think you want to hear. It's a tactic they use to get women to trust them. What other proof do you need to understand that some guys are just plain heartless? These types of guys only care about what you can do for them at that moment. But your life, legacy, and dreams are far more important than a scumbag who does not care anything about you.

My advice to you is to focus on school or anything else besides a guy that will make you better as a woman. Anybody who takes your attention or energy away from your goals is somebody you should stay away from. If they drain your energy, make you feel tired or lazy because of their constant arguing, or give off other types of negative energy, get them out of your life and never look back. You are important and should demand respect. If you don't demand this for yourself, you're setting yourself up to get hurt and that pain will follow you for the rest of your life.

Always remember your main focus should be your future. There's no time for drama. You've got to keep it moving, and if that means letting friends go, then so be it. Everything that wants to survive must evolve. Plants, animals, and humans. Nobody is safe unless they stay ahead of the game, including you. Now, you don't need to worry just yet because you've already got a leg up by reading this book.

A man can only do what you allow him to do, so don't fall victim to his foolishness. You are a Goddess. You can create life! You are the only pathway to continuing the existence of the human race in this world. It's critical that you understand how important and valuable you are. Never let anyone tell you anything different. Leave any guy who causes stress in your life or who influences you to act out of character. Once you allow someone to change you, you will begin to question yourself and that is not healthy at all.

If he does not truly care for you, he will lead you down the wrong path in such a way that you will be dependent on his words to guide you out. Women who allow this to happen may be setting themselves up to be controlled. The way he will try to rebuild your relationship with fake apologies may seem sweet.

There may only be twenty-six letters in the alphabet, but the combinations of words he chooses strategically will sound like the sweetest melodies a woman could ever hear. But we all know nothing sounds better than the truth. Remember, you don't need a man to tell you who you are. This is something you should already know before you enter a relationship. Knowing what you're worth and what you value in life, and staying true to those things will ultimately prevent any guy from being able to control you by playing with your emotions. You don't want to be in a position where you feel so lonely you're willing talk to someone who you know deep down you should not be talking to. One way to help prevent that is to focus your time and attention on taking care of yourself instead of spending time with a guy who hasn't earned your trust yet. Take some time and go to a nice spa or plan an outdoor adventure like hiking or zip lining with a friend or family member. Go on a vacation. Listen to some music that puts you in a good mood. Spend more time with family. I know a few women who purchased a puppy to help them get over a breakup. They all said the genuine feeling of loyalty and love that the dog gave back to them as it got older was soothing.

Preying on a woman's loneliness is a strategy that can be very dangerous for many reasons. Players understand when a woman is experiencing loneliness after a breakup. The possibility she is only using him to get over her ex doesn't bother a player at all because he sees it as an opportunity. In a player's mind, his main goal is to get her mind off of her ex. Players understand a lot of women will have their guard down momentarily. The player's objective is to see what he can get out of the situation as well.

A woman's confidence is a very powerful thing. I feel it's made up of the experiences she has had in her childhood and past. These might include a good memory from childhood or the values and principles her parents instilled in her from a young age or any negative situation when she had to endure pain. A few examples could be bad relationships and friendships or any situation that involved anxiety and stress. The beauty of these past mishaps is how people grow and learn from them. That is where wisdom and value thrives. We become smarter, stronger emotionally, and more focused when we learn from difficult experiences. In my opinion, wisdom is what we learn from our mistakes in order to bring about better outcomes in the future. The value lies within yourself. A young woman must know her confidence is much more than the makeup and expensive heels she wears. Your confidence also dictates your present and future. You should cherish and protect your confidence as a gift from God. Many say men should fear nothing but God. That's why I think most men are afraid to approach real women with true confidence. I guarantee most men are afraid to even make eye contact for long periods of time with a woman who has confidence. It's almost as if he knows she can see through his lies.

I believe this is the reason many successful and powerful women have a hard time finding a man. But this is nothing to be sad about. In fact, be thankful because you don't have to waste your time, which is a valuable commodity, remember? The men who can't handle your confidence and are too afraid to take you seriously are not real men, only decoys to slow you down in life. Never let a man try to break down your confidence when in fact he was never the source of it in the first place.

7

The very same guy who was afraid to look you in the eyes will try to find a so-called insecure woman only to take advantage of her. In reality, he's looking for all the things he doesn't have. Some guys may say hurtful things if they can't get their way or if they realize you are finally tired and leaving them for all the things they put you through.

They will try to insult you and say stuff like you are ugly and nobody else will ever want to be with you. *Nobody will ever marry you. Nobody will put up with your attitude.* Do not fall for these manipulation tactics. They may also make disparaging remarks about your body or bring up things from your past that you are uncomfortable talking about. He is trying to play off your emotions and get a reaction out of you. Do not pay attention to this immature behavior.

You are beautiful, smart, funny, and have so many other qualities that he will never get to experience because you will not tolerate any disrespect! After he says all the mean, hurtful things to you and some time passes, he will try to be nice to you again. If a woman goes through this over and over (keep in mind it will never change), she will begin to operate as if the verbal abuse is normal behavior.

That's why it's important to get away from negativity as quickly as possible. Don't ever let a man abuse you physically or emotionally. Once they show you the hateful, disrespectful side of themselves, leave and don't look back ever again. Love yourself first. Do not wait until it's too late because you may pick up some of his negative traits or harbor resentment against all men because of what you experienced with him. If that's the case, you may run a good man off because of your previous bad relationship. It's not worth it.

Do not change your personality for anyone. Don't be afraid to be yourself. There's no point in worrying about someone else's opinion of you. If you are not 100 percent happy in a relationship or situation, you have the right to leave and should. Do not feel bad for leaving. You will feel better after you leave, which is most important. The time is now.

The Games Men Play

Be careful and watch out for guys who are willing to tell you anything they think you want to hear. The creepy part is that these kinds of guys will spot you before you even see them coming. Men will tell you what they think they want to hear in the hopes of putting you at ease so that you'll let your guard down. Then they can slip in and begin controlling your mind as if you were under the spell of a master puppeteer.

Once he invades your mind, he will attempt to control your body. Remember, your body is a sacred vessel. You have a connection with a higher dimension that allows you to give life. You must protect and carry yourself in an elite manner no matter what is thrown your way.

Most guys you meet are no different than parasites camouflaged in good looks and friendly smiles. What purpose does a guy like that have in your life? These types only want to manipulate and take advantage of you. Never lose focus of your goals. Most men will do and say anything that they think will make you feel comfortable around them. They are not going to approach you with a shirt that reads, "I'm here to manipulate you and slow you down in life." So, be on the lookout. In this section, I offer several examples of the strategies men use to control and influence women that may seem harmless to the naked eye but in reality can be damaging to women.

Men Want You to Do All the Talking

Let's say you're currently in a relationship and you meet a guy at school, work, gym, etc. He approaches you and you explain to him that you're in a relationship. What was your initial reason for speaking to him in the first place? Did you speak to him because he asked you a question? Why did you feel the need to explain your situation to a random guy you know nothing about?

There's nothing wrong with speaking to someone if he says hello or good morning. If he gets upset because you choose not to carry on conversation with him, that's his own personal problem. Maybe you are not in the mood to be bothered. If you come off as bitchy, then so be it. Who is he to say you don't have a right to be? Maybe a woman is tired of scumbags approaching her. A man has no choice but to respect that. A woman should never feel obligated to speak to a man to avoid upsetting him. You must understand that just because a guy speaks to you, that doesn't mean he automatically deserves any of your conversation or attention. I suggest you choose the guy you want to talk to, instead of waiting for a guy to talk to you. Do your homework on him first. Watch and observe. Analyze if he is a good fit for your life by engaging him in a brief conversation.

Some men will respect the fact that you're in a relationship and back off. This is no big deal because you are attractive inside and out. But a lot of women don't realize that he is counting on running into you again, probably in the same place, especially if you two met at school. It bothers him that you didn't fall for his game like the other girls. You become an object of desire, a challenge to overcome in his wicked thoughts that still burn with rejection.

He's not concerned with the fact that you didn't give him attention in the beginning. You will run into him again, I guarantee it, because it's a strategy that men have been using for decades, if not centuries. The other thing you need to know is that if he was bold enough to approach you, trust that he is talking to other women as well. You are not the first girl that he thought was attractive. Some men view talking to beautiful women as a challenge or confidence builder. The more confidence he has the more courage he will muster to speak to multiple women in any given day.

No matter how good his words sound, know that you are not the only woman he's got his eye on. From now on, every time you see him he will only say hi and smile at you. Eventually, he will stop talking to you all together. Now in this case, his sudden lack of interest will leave some women wondering, "What is wrong with me? Why isn't he paying attention to me?" It's all strategy. Stand your ground and don't pay him any mind.

Timing Is Just a Waiting Game

Weeks go by, maybe even months. You and the guy you're currently dating may have a disagreement to the point where you are not on speaking terms. The next day, you stumble across the same guy whom you explained your relationship status to previously. He speaks to you again because he notices something different about you. Maybe it's your hair, clothing, or the extra time you've been spending at the gym.

Let's say this time you decide to hear him out. In his mind, he figures you either broke up with your boyfriend or are on bad terms, but either way he does not care because he is out to conquer. His objective hasn't changed. This change is obvious to him because you are actually giving him attention. You must remember, it's not just the romantic guys in novels and movies who pay close attention to women. Players and smooth talkers are watching and waiting as well.

He will try to play the laid back funny guy, hoping to put a smile on your face. The majority of the time this strategy works because we all enjoy a good laugh. There will be times in your life when all you want to do is take your mind off the current situation with your boyfriend or stressful issues in your day-to-day life.

If you are not careful, the negative energy from stress will cause a chain reaction of events you could never imagine. That's why you must remain focused and aware of yourself at all times no matter how you are feeling emotionally. An emotion is just that an emotion whether you're sad or happy, laughing or crying. One is not greater than the other. You wouldn't laugh all day, every day, for weeks in a row because people would probably start to question whether you are still mentally there. So why be upset or sad for just as long? You must be able to think rationally at all times. Never let your guard down.

A lot of guys prey upon women who are fresh out of a relationship or have problems in their relationships. Relationship problems are always great news to the guys lying in wait. Imagine them excited to tell all their friends about your situation. The first thing out of their mouths would be, "So you know what that means." They are anticipating that the woman will not be able to think rationally, which means it will be easier to take advantage of her mind.

If you find yourself in this situation, you will be viewed as vulnerable and an easy mission to accomplish. As men, we understand that the majority of women going through a breakup just want to take their minds off of it. So when we see clues that all is not well in a woman's relationship, men see a window of opportunity to take advantage of that situation. If you're fresh out of a relationship, I recommend that you take time to heal first. If you don't, you will easily end up as a tally mark on some poor excuse of a man's hit list.

You will only feel worse in the end and have more problems to deal with, so don't fall for the lies spilling out of that smooth talker's mouth. Now that you understand the strategy he will try to use, you can stay alert and watch out for this kind of behavior. From your point of view, you may have labeled him as a friend and think it's fine for the conversation and laughter to continue. A smooth-talking man doesn't mind waiting it out, so he is comfortable in the friend zone.

Keep in mind some of the most poisonous snakes in the world will wait long periods of time for their prey before striking them dead at the blink of an eye. Then they slowly slither away to the next victim with no emotions in their body and even more confidence running through their veins.

A Man in Demand Holds All the Cards

In school, many girls may have a crush on athletes or the popular guy. You must realize those type of guys have girls chasing them all the time. The likelihood of getting your heart broken is very high.

For example, a guy like that already knows that he has many options and probably talks to more women daily than the average man. His status puts him in a position where girls will lie about relationships they're in or may stay in contact with him in order to stay in his life for their own personal gain. These women are willing to lie for him and help protect what they may be doing secretly behind his girlfriend's or wife's back. Although a shot at being his girlfriend or wife is not guaranteed, they are willing to take the risk.

Never give a guy any of your time if he gives a lot of other girls his time and attention. You must demand more respect. Otherwise, he will walk all over you or act as if you don't exist until the day he decides you are relevant again. It sounds crazy, but sadly this is true. Throughout your high school and college years you are simply a goal in a boy's eyes.

That goal is driven by his hormones, which gives him a one-track mind. Ask yourself a question. Do you really want to be the girl who gave up something so precious to a guy who doesn't care for you and only wants sex? Trust me, you are far more important than his mind can comprehend. You should be interested in the guy for the right reasons as well. If you are only going off of his looks and muscular build, you're setting yourself up for things to move a lot faster than normal if you don't have self control because you are already physically attracted to him. I'm well aware that there are a lot of women out there who enjoy sex just as much as men. But you are worth more than locker room talk—and that is exactly what will happen. He will brag to other people about how he got to you first and use a lot of other disrespectful and derogatory language. There's a good chance everyone in the school will find out. That's where the rumors begin, so just avoid it. Don't fall for the trap.

The Three Letters He Uses to Get to Your Heart

Before I go any further, I must explain the A.C.T. strategy, which stands for attention, comfort, and trust. These are the routes a womanizer will take to a woman's heart. He will be able to make it through all the check points with red flags undetected. If you give him attention, it will be full speed ahead to Comfort Avenue.

Women feel comfortable when they can be themselves around a guy. All the laughter and goofiness may seem like a dream come true. He answers every text and call from you. You are getting all the attention in the world, it may seem. Now, almost like clockwork, you begin to trust him.

Imagine walking into a huge cobweb in the middle of the night. You might remove the web and think nothing else of it. But what if a spider crawls into your hair during the process? The majority of people will never see it until it's too late. View a man's words as if they were spider webs. You never know what's lurking in them.

Some guys are hoping that you feel some type of emotion from your so-called "friendship." I guarantee you will develop some feelings for him if you spend enough time together or communicate on the phone often.

Once you begin to call or text more frequently, in his mind he has you right where he wants you. Some women may think this is the sign of a sweet guy because he hasn't brought anything up about sex. He doesn't even mention it and it has been over a month or two of texting and phone calls. Please don't be fooled by these ploys and overlook the dark side of a gentlemen.

The side you've seen of him is well groomed. He uses eye contact like a language. A man can easily put the mask of a perfect gentleman on. Some women think that if a man shows generosity he automatically identifies with what it truly means to be a good guy. That simple mistake will allow an imposter to infiltrate your magic. The gentlemen with a sense of humor and business about himself can communicate with four to twenty females easily within a day's time.

I remember waking up one morning and sending a mass text to ten to fifteen women. "Good morning, I've been thinking about you lately." They didn't know I sent the same text to multiple women. They assumed it was only them, yet they all replied back with similar messages.

I'm talking about the same guy who makes you laugh and smile. This is one of many reasons most guys do not bring up sex at all during the first few months or possibly even years. It's because all the other women he talks to are on different frequencies in his mind and he treats them accordingly. More than likely he is having sex with quite a few of them. Of course, he didn't meet all of them on the same day, but I promise you it's possible for him to meet just as many women in one day. Especially if he is a popular athlete, that number could double within weeks. He categorizes the women so that the ones with highest priority come first. That priority will vary depending on how he sees fit. A smart man knows that the majority of women want the same thing: time, which is priceless. I'm not talking about the men that sit around all day without anything productive to do. Those are the type you should never give any attention to. Any successful woman who is financially stable values her time. The same thing goes for a successful man. Successful people are usually busy working hard. So when they do have a little time to spare, they would rather spend it wisely rather than with someone who has nothing to do all day. Men without goals who are not productive have a lot of time because they are not doing anything in life. Obviously, guys like this are dead weight. They have all the time in the world to offer. Don't make a deal with the devil. If he is not valuing his own time by doing productive work, what makes you think he will value yours?

Some men will try to make you feel as if you owe them something. This is an attempt to make you feel guilty. He needs some type of leverage, in his mind, to gain control of the situation. Others will try to use their power, status, and money to intimidate you. Don't ever let someone talk you into doing something you don't want to do, or something that you know is not right.

A New Breed of Players

You are not dealing with players from back in the day. Today's players are men who have older brothers, cousins, and uncles who taught them game at a very young age. In some cases, even their fathers will pass this curse on to their sons. I used to observe the strategies of old-school players and pay attention to the ones that didn't work. I was more interested in their failures. I recalculated their steps. Analyzed their approach. I decided to eradicate all arrogance on my part as if it was hazmat. As if I was a chemist, I singled out truth and loyalty as the scientific elements guaranteed to win women over. The truth is the only thing women want to hear. I used this knowledge to my benefit—to separate myself from regular players—and found myself in a league of my own. Ladies, please be aware that the men out there today are not old-school players, but a new breed of players who have learned from the old-schooler's mistakes.

There is a new code that we move by: eye contact. I believe eye contact is powerful enough to stop time, softer than a whisper, yet loud enough to transfer thoughts. That is how this new breed is able to have conversations with other women while on a date with you unnoticed. Eye contact is hard to track because you won't know to look for the signs unless you understand it.

Eye Contact Is a Powerful Tool for Capturing a Woman's Attention

One day I was having dinner with a young lady. I remember it like it was yesterday. The parking lot was full when we pulled up to the restaurant. Luckily, she made reservations because if it was up to me we would have been waiting like the people we passed on the way in with angry looks on their faces. We were greeted at the door by a young, energetic hostess. She smiled at us and we followed her, making a zigzag to our seats.

"I noticed the waitress checking you out," my date said. "She was probably wondering how a man like me got with a good-looking woman like you," I answered. Then I proceeded to compliment her attire.

It's crucial that you understand guys can play with words as if they were lawyers. You must find something else that makes him special rather than the sweet things he says to you. If he wasn't saying it to you, he would be telling the same thing to another woman. The problem is men will use a combination of compliments to hypnotize a woman and paralyze her defenses. Things will not end in your favor.

We proceeded to enjoy our appetizers while we waited for the chef to prepare our dinner. I noticed a group of women sitting at a table across from us. All of them were laughing and having a good time, it seemed, except one particular lady. In fact, she wasn't paying any attention to her friends at all. Her eyes were locked with mine for a few seconds before breaking eye contact. I glanced at my date as I was ready to defend myself with lies if she had noticed. She had no idea and was looking at the menu, anticipating dessert. I grinned with a sigh of relief. It was game on.

After a sip of my drink, I glanced back over to the table with the lady I had made eye contact with earlier. I wanted to see if I could get her attention without anyone noticing. It worked. Our eye contact ended this time with a slight smile from both of us as if we were the only two people who knew the biggest secret in the world. I needed a plan and fast, so I told my date I was going to the restroom to wash my hands before our food arrived. I excused myself and headed straight to the bathroom. On the way to the restroom I had to walk by the lady I was flirting with. My intention was to get her attention as I walked by. Somehow, I had to figure out how to pull this off without getting caught and divulging my ulterior motives.

When I walked by their table, to my surprise she already had her eyes on me. This was becoming easier than I imagined. I smiled and continued walking by as if nothing had happened. When I made it to the restroom, I washed my hands, dried them off, and looked in the mirror. I checked my phone to see the time and had a few missed calls from other women. I sent a text back to every woman I had a missed called from. I told them all the same thing: "I'm eating dinner with my parents and will call soon as I'm done." Then I put my phone in my pocket after I made sure the ringer was off and still on vibrate.

I left the bathroom and noticed the lady I was flirting with headed my way. My plan worked. She had excused herself to the restroom as well. I introduced myself to her with a fake name and told her I was there with my sister to celebrate her birthday. "You should come sing happy birthday to her," I said as we both laughed. My intention was to throw off any thought she may have had that I was there on a date. I mentioned that my food had probably arrived at the table by now, so I should get going. "That is sweet of you taking your sister out for her birthday," she said and told me to type her number into my phone and call her sometime. I typed her number in and told her I would call later after I took my sister home.

A lot of women think they are in control when it comes to men, but they are not aware that they are being manipulated from the start. I headed back to my table hoping my date hadn't seen me or noticed anything out of the ordinary. When I got back, the waitress was at the table with our food. Everything seemed normal until I saw the lady whose number I had just gotten walking towards us.

We made eye contact as she got closer. I wasn't sure if she was actually coming to sing happy birthday or not, but a blanket of fear covered me and my food became instantly hard to swallow. The room felt as if it was closing in on me. Ten million things ran through my mind all at once. *How will I be able to get out of this one?* was the last question that ran through my mind. I was ready to fall out of my chair and hit the floor as if I was choking. Any distraction that would take light off the situation. I took a huge bite of steak and prepared for the ride.

Thankfully, I was safe once again. She didn't come to my table. She sat back at her own table with her friends and continued the rest of her evening. The lady I exchanged numbers with had no idea what I was up to and neither did my date. It was a huge relief to me. The majority of women make it easy for guys to cheat and lie to them because all they do is talk about themselves the entire time.

Honeyed Words Cast a Sticky Web

I need you to keep in mind that if you never met this guy, he would be telling another girl the same sweet things he says to you. Any guy can strategically put words together to form a compliment or joke to make a woman smile. Ask yourself, how important are compliments?

Sure, compliments are nice to hear, but you must love yourself first before anyone else can truly love you. You are a Queen who refuses to tolerate anything less than respect because disrespect is toxic to your empire. The first weapon he uses is merely his presence. My cologne catches a lot of ladies' attentions. I've had women hunt me down in public numerous times just to ask me what type of cologne I was wearing. I understand how powerful scent can be because it can cause instant attraction. That's the main reason I started collecting colognes. Eye contact comes next. Words are usually the third weapon he will use to chip away at your defenses. You do not need validation from anyone to remind you who you are.

One way to help prevent a guy from using his words to charm you is to avoid flirting a lot and coming off as too nice. Being overly friendly is an invitation to have games played on you. A man instantly feels as if he is in control at that point. This is where the lies will breach your system. While he's flirting with you he will allow you to think whatever you want about him, as long as you're not aware of the fact that it is actually you who is being analyzed.

He Pulls Back When He Wants to Reel You In

The majority of fake relationships are mostly about mind control in the beginning. Guys will never admit it, which is I'm about to tell it all. Negative energy is passed to a woman and then hijacks her mind during a heated disagreement. The gateway is usually your cellphone. For example, you may not want other women calling or texting his phone and he may say the people texting him are his friends. Once he knows you are upset or trying to get your point across, he most likely will hang up on you. He is betting on you calling him right back and he will not pick up. He knows you want to get your point across but refuses to let you by not answering your call.

Do not text during this time because you will get short, unsatisfying responses if any at all. The negative energy between you will be multiplied that way.

If a guy hangs up on you, do not call back no matter how hard it may be to resist. Never let a man calculate your steps, especially if his intentions are bad. If he hangs up the phone with no logical reason, wait until he calls you. Depending on his experience level, you may not be the first girl he's tried this strategy on. Remember, this is a battle of energy you are dealing with. If you don't handle this kind of situation carefully, it will cause you to lose focus on your day-to-day activities.

Players understand a lot of women love attention. For example, if a woman gets compliments or attention all the time in public or on social media, there's a good chance she will become dependent on this form of feedback. Out of 100 guys, she may receive 99 good compliments, but the one guy who ignored her gets the most attention from her. In her mind, she is wondering why he isn't drooling over her like the rest of the men. Imagine if he hangs up on her and doesn't call back right away. Hours go by. This is something new to her. She isn't getting her way. Who does he think he is? Almost like clockwork, she begins to chase him. Although she may have 49 guys chasing after her, begging to be her knight in shining armor, there's always at least one guy who really sparks her interest because he isn't willing to cooperate. That is what I call someone who is from the new breed of players—a hybrid.

Unnecessary stress is not something you want in your life. If you feel a strong urge to call the guy back and get your point across, that means you're holding onto that negative energy. However, now that I've explained this kind of behavior, it should be easier for you to let pass. You are already a step ahead of him. You understand the type of mind games that are being played so laugh it off and don't call or send a text message. The amount of time you have been talking to each other will determine the amount of time it takes before he calls you back. If you just started talking to the guy, he wont call back too fast. He is trying to prove a point, as if you are not needed in his life. It's a tactic he's using. This is done in the hope that she will attempt to call or text him first.

If you've been talking to him for less than a month, it's even more critical that you do not call or text him first. The first month is when he is trying to gain power over you through the energy he sends. Usually he will not call or send a text until ten minutes or up to one hour has passed. After fifteen minutes have gone by, he will start to feel the same negative energy you felt earlier. During this small window of opportunity, it's important for the woman to stand firm. Every player knows he could possibly lose the greatest thing that may have ever happened to him. It's a gamble every time that he is willing to take. But if he knows he is in the wrong, he may become afraid of losing a good woman. Keep in mind you should be smiling because you are aware of his game and the ball is in your court.

He may text you something crazy or disrespectful. Do not fall for this strategy. He does that only to get under your skin. He is trying to get some type of response from you. Do not participate in these games. It's a desperate attempt to send back the negative energy he's feeling. In reality, he's actually wondering why you haven't called or texted back like he was anticipating.

He is trying to manipulate and run game on you, so his mind starts to wonder as his plan backfires. *What is she doing right now? Why hasn't she called back? Who is she talking to or texting on the phone?* Now he's concerned and wondering if he went too far and lost a good woman. These are just a few of many questions that are putting his mind in overdrive.

He has no idea you are reading this book, which has given you an inside look on every possible game a guy will try to play. When he finally calls you back, just play it smooth as if you are unbothered and haven't noticed how much time has gone by. It may sound crazy, but some guys like women to chase them. They do this because it helps boost their ego. Never let a man use you as a stepping stone. Trust me, they will use you if you allow them to.

I suggest you don't pick up the first time he calls back. Wait until the sixth or seventh time he calls. He is on your time, you are not on his. If he tries to send an apology through text do not reply. Never reply back to a text during a situation like this. Make him call back a few times before answering. Once you become comfortable with the strategy, don't pick up the phone until the next day. Let him suffer.

When he finally calls back again and you pick up, he better be talking respectful with a sincere apology. If he ever tries to play that game again, I suggest you leave him alone completely. He is not ready mentally to settle down. He wants to be in control and run circles around you. Remember, a man should jump through hoops to make you smile. You are a gift in his life and he is an option in yours.

You have to trust a guy before you can love him. If you fall for him before you build that trust with him, it's almost guaranteed he will betray you in some form or fashion, which you will never find out about.

The Friend Zone Is the Danger Zone
Another category a guy will try to put you in without your knowledge is the friend zone. I can promise you thousands and thousands of women have experienced what I'm about to describe and they wish they could take it all back.

When a man is in the friend zone, he's able to do what he wants as far as talking to or dating other women. He does not have to abide by any relationship guidelines. In his mind if you're just a friend, he can have sex with you without having to be your husband or in any type of relationship. He doesn't have to answer when you call or be faithful to you, which means he will be talking to other women. To him, you are just a sex object to use with no commitment. Trust that he will never tell you that, but it's definitely in the back of his mind. He will go on casual dates with you and listen to your problems about other people.

Do not catch feelings for a guy you put in the friend zone. It's too risky. You will eventually tell him everything that went on in your previous relationship because you are slowly letting your guard down without realizing it. More than likely, the guy you are calling your friend will readily agree with everything you say about it.

He will agree with you even if you are wrong in the situation you described to him. You don't need people like that around you. His motive is to gain your trust quickly and become more sympathetic in your eyes. He knows you are probably hurting from that previous relationship. For a woman who has no idea what's going, this will seem like normal behavior. But in reality, you are jeopardizing your health, emotions, mind, energy, and sanity if you allow this type of nonsense to go on. This type of behavior goes unnoticed a lot of the time because some women think the guy truly wants to be their friend. Just because you can call him when you need someone to talk to does not exempt him from having ulterior motives.

Some guys will invent a story to make it seem as if they went through the same exact scenario you did. For example, if you told him you broke up with your previous boyfriend for cheating, he may say that's the same reason he broke up with his girlfriend. As he listens to your complaints from your previous relationship, he may morph into your ideal man momentarily.

Players pray on women in weak moments when they're going through a breakup, divorce, or heated disagreements with current boyfriend or husband. Every move from these young players is calculated as if it was a venomous snake bite. He will look deep into your eyes and lie with no remorse. Don't ever let a lie hide behind charm and good looks.

Although no woman deserves to be treated as such, it's important to realize most men will not be faithful until they are finally ready and willing to be faithful on their own terms. There's nothing you can say or do that will change his mind. He will agree with you and your reasoning for the time being, but nothing will change. It's only a tactic to prevent you from discussing a particular altercation any further.

He Crafts His Appearance to Deceive You

Here's another example of a common pitfall in dating. If a man is well dressed all the time or drives a nice car, you may think that he has a lot of money and is successful. How can you determine a guy is successful without knowing what his definition of success is? I can assure you right, success is not determined by materialistic things. A lot of men live their lives pretending to be successful and financially stable because they understand many women are attracted to that lifestyle.

Never come to a conclusion about a guy based on your first impression of his looks, the way he dresses, the car he drives, or other superficial attributes. Guys will spend their last dollar buying cars, clothes, and anything else in the hopes of impressing a woman. There's a good chance he is not financially responsible if he spends money that way.

Women, you are setting yourselves up to fall short in the end if you make your calculations of a man's character based on his material possessions. If a man's value is rooted in the things he owns, what value does he have to you as a person in a relationship? Any guy can save up enough money to buy designer clothing, shoes, and fancy cars to appear as if he is financially stable. Don't fall victim to this false front.

He Uses Words to Evade Your Detection

If a guy tells you he's talking to someone, what does that mean to you? You must make a man clarify that statement! I told you earlier to always question everything. If a woman does not clarify the things a man says, then he has many escape routes from a lie if he ever gets caught in one.

Even though he knows that when he says he's "talking to someone" that means he's dating someone, he could easily switch up the definition later if need be. I will give you one of many examples. If a guy meets a woman for the first time and they start dating, he can dismiss any questions she asks regarding his previous relationships or about the woman he currently talks to by saying, "She wasn't important, we were just talking." He says this as if he is just brushing her off.

A man will withhold key pieces of information unless you ask specific questions that force him to reveal the exact details. Most operate on a "don't ask, don't tell" policy, which means if you don't ask the right questions you will never know. Even if you do ask the right questions, you will probably not get a true answer from a young player. All players have a way with words. You'll have to damn near catch him in the act or get him on camera, and even then he will deny it. The only way to catch him is to remember his answers to your questions. Write them down in a diary if you have to. It will be hard for him to remember a lie he told a week ago, especially since most lies have to be covered up with more lies to sound real.

After a few days or maybe even weeks pass, ask him the same questions again, but in a slightly different way. You have to camouflage the questions. For example, let's say your husband tells you he is attending a football game tonight with the guys so you shouldn't stay up late, but he actually goes to another woman's house. How can you find out the truth? A few days later ask him who won the game (you already did your research and know the answer.) A few days later ask him what time the game started (you already know the time he left). Only ask questions you already know the answers to or the answers he told you. I know this seems like a lot to do, but trust me it's worth it. There is no room for toxic situations or people in your life.

Cheaters Are Experts in the Art of Lying

There are more guys out there who cheat and don't get caught than there are guys who cheat and do get caught. Only the rookies get caught. For example, let's say you meet a guy and you both introduce yourselves. He seems like a nice guy, so you exchange numbers. You talk on the phone with him for hours just about every other day. Months pass by of getting to know each other in this way and everything seems to be going just fine. You haven't decided to date him yet, but your feelings for him are getting stronger and you can't hide it. Before you know it, you are in a relationship.

But realize this: it's possible that you were being played from the start. Do you remember when you first met him? In your mind, he's the one. You've been telling your family about him and bragging about him to your friends.

You have no idea that he gave you a fake name. How can you trace anything back to him if that's the case? Some women are so mesmerized by a guy's eyes, looks, car, or clothes, or his way with words, that they let their guards down. The signs were obvious, but they choose to ignore them.

Something as simple as a name could cost you everything. He could be married or in an on-going relationship, but you will never find out if you believe everything that he says without questioning it.

A guy can date many different women in the same city and never get caught because he gives all of them different names and never his real name. I know it seems far-fetched, but I promise this happens and women have no idea.

Remember when you gave him your name and number to save in his phone? He saved your information under one of his male friends' names so that your call will go under the radar when he's with other women. Of course, he chose a male friend's name that begins with the same letter as yours, so he doesn't forget your name and get you confused with someone else.. For example, if your name is Laura, he will save it as Lance. If your name is Brittany, he will save it as Brandon. I'm sure you get my point. You could be calling him while he is sitting beside his girlfriend and neither of you will never know. This is only the tip of the iceberg.

Some men play the game on an even higher level by only talking to women that live in different cities. This lowers his odds of getting caught red handed. Imagine how complex it is to keep tabs on a man who travels out of state regularly, such as the average professional athlete, businessman, entertainer, truck driver, etc. Even if he lives with his girlfriend or wife, when he's on the road and far away from home he can participate in sketch activities without his woman ever finding out.

I'm sure some ladies are reading this and thinking there's no way their man could be cheating because they know his schedule like clockwork. They may even have the password to his phone. Let me ask you a few questions. How hard is it to get a cheap, pre-paid phone for around twenty to thirty dollars? You know, the same cheap phones that most people laugh at when they see them. How hard is it to put a fake name on that account? I promise it won't even take him 15 minutes to do that. Most women are satisfied when their man lets them go through his phone and think they have the perfect guy. Little do they know that pre-paid flip phones hold all the information they need to catch him and expose him for who he truly is.

The problem is I guarantee that phone is nowhere in sight. It will be in a place that he thinks his woman will never look, like the toolbox, fishing tackle box, car trunk, old shoes in a closet, etc. This new breed of players takes it a step further and hides the phone at a family member's house or in the woods.

These guys will even separate the battery from the phone in case and hide them in two different spots just to be on the safe side. You can't turn the phone on without the battery and a battery without a phone is no good either. If you luck out and find both pieces, guess what? The sim card is missing as well.

A true player understands that staying on top of the game is a full-time job doing. They will go to extreme measures to keep their secret life under control. Even if the innocent lady he is cheating with finds out about his girlfriend or wife and decides to expose him. What evidence does she have?

I'm sure you're thinking, "Well, maybe she has a few texts and phone calls that prove his cheating." I hate to say it, but he has out smarted the situation once again. Remember the phone is not in his name and, on top of that, his current girlfriend or wife has never seen him with another phone.

Plus, the woman who is trying to expose him is calling him by a different name. Remember, he gave her a fake name from the start in case something like this ever happened. Now this lady seems crazy because she isn't even calling him by his right name.

He tells his wife or girlfriend that it must be one of his ex's friends trying to destroy what you two have built together. As soon as he gets the chance, he will call customer service and tell them he is getting harassment calls to that pre-paid number. He changes the number or throws the phone away and gets a new one altogether—and the cycle continues. One thing he will not do is continue talking to the woman who tried to expose him. This is similar to the way a billionaire writes a loss off on their taxes and moves on to the next thing.

I'm not saying this is guaranteed to happen to you. I'm only saying that it happens every day. Divorce attorneys make a huge profit off infidelity. It's how they make a living and feed their families. So that should tell you something.

He Wants Your Emotions to Get the Better of You

If you find yourself in this kind of situation with a man, remain calm. I know that's easier said than done. It's understandable that you might be angry and hurt by such a discovery. But try to stay unemotional and logical about your next steps. The absolute worst thing you can do is continue to engage with negative energy, which will slow you down in life. Do not retaliate in any fashion. Please do not do anything that will put you in jail or impact your career and money. While you're stuck in jail, he will be free to continue doing the very same thing that made you lose your composure in the first place. He will continue living his dishonest life, and trust that he will not be thinking of you. Your best revenge is success and happiness. I promise you he will regret his dishonesty in the end.

Never give him the chance to get close to you ever again. That means do not let that man back into your life no matter how many times he apologizes because what he did was not an innocent mistake, it was intentional. You cannot put his actions in the same category as a child spilling a drink or a toddler feeding the family pet ice cream and bubble gum. This is a young adult who knows better. He was very aware of what he was doing and realized it was wrong, but dismissed your feelings anyway. He is probably only sorry that you found out and caught him. Keep it moving because time waits for nobody, so you don't have any to waste on him.

Two Wrongs Won't Make It Right

Nothing good comes from jealousy, resentment, or lust. In this day and age, you can't even trust your neighbor or roommate 100 percent of the time. A lot of women make the mistake of trying to retaliate for infidelity by cheating as well. They will only regret it in the end because they will become the type of woman who helps guys cheat.

I will put myself in a scenario to help you better understand. For example, let's say a woman decides to cheat with me because she is in an emotional spiral and wants to get back at her man for cheating on her. This is a situation where it's easy for me to take advantage of her. All I have to do is agree with everything she says and give her a shoulder to lean on. My next move is simply telling her everything she wants to hear. A player realizes she is letting her guard down. There's a certain type of guy who preys upon women who have been hurt. These men are no different than the type of women some call "homewreckers." These are ladies who are aware that a man already has a wife or girlfriend but still pursue him anyway.

A player will easily sit back and wait on a woman to get out of a marriage or relationship while manipulating her under the radar. Only lower level players who are inexperienced come off as rude and disrespectful when approaching a woman. Advanced, experienced players are respectful, humble, and a lot smarter.

He Uses Comparison to Make You Feel Insecure

Some men may also try to make you jealous of another woman. Maybe he will bring up his ex in comparison to you . That's a sign. For example, maybe she didn't complain or worry about some of the things you complain and worry about. Trust me there is nothing wrong with you.

Another line they may use is, "My ex helped me out financially. Can you lend me some money?" Your response should be, "I'm not your ex," and leave it at that. He is only trying to make you feel guilty. If you just met the guy and he already has his hand out, you should blink twice, clap your hands, and try hard to teleport away from him as quick as possible.

He may also try to act as if other women text or call his phone all the time. This is a strategy to make you move faster. He wants you to feel like you're competing for his attention and that you should feel lucky he is in your life. He may be using this strategy to convince you to have sex with him or to force you into a relationship. Either way it's a form of manipulation.

Maybe he will lie and say a lot of women are after him to make it seem as if he is a great catch. He's betting on your next move. He wants to be ahead of you mentally and his choice of words camouflage his ulterior motives. Ask yourself why you want to talk to or date a man that every woman wants? Think about all the stress and worrying you will experience. If a lot of women are chasing him, eventually a few will catch him when you are not around.

You will lose yourself in the mix of all the madness. Don't ever put yourself in a position or relationship where you will constantly worry about what someone may be doing behind your back. A guy will also use the eye contact strategy we talked about earlier—the language of lost words. As I mentioned earlier, if I know a woman recently got out of a relationship, more than likely she is hurting and vulnerable. You must remember a guy will play any role he feels necessary at a particular time. If a woman suggests that I might be taking advantage of her emotional state of mind, all I would have to do is pretend that I'm shocked and say I just got hurt or cheated on as well.

Any player can easily make up a story that he thinks you can relate off the top of his head. Only a rookie would say the exact same thing you told him happened to him. The guys you need to watch out for are the ones who make themselves out to be the victim before you tell them about your situation. He brings up his own breakup early in the conversation because he is hoping the reason you are single is because you got hurt.

Once you catch on to what he is doing, turn the questions back on him. Do not give him the chance to question you because that's how he takes control of the conversation. You must play it smart and smooth. You can even turn his questions back on to him. I will give a few examples. You can ask him, "How old are you?" After he tells you his age, crack a joke like, "You don't look your age, so how do I know you are over eighteen?" Ask him what year he was born to see if the age he told you matches up correctly. The hope is that he'll show you his license. If he does, you can check his real name, age, and where he is from. (Let's hope its not a fake ID.) If you do it this way, there is a greater chance his strategy will malfunction because you have caught him off guard and are keeping him on his toes. Be sure to make strong eye contact and pay close attention to his movements. His lies will bleed through his skin.

Dating is like playing against an undefeated team in the Super Bowl. You and your team and you have done just enough to barely make it there because you were hit hard along the way. You may have taken a lot of losses in the past. You may have gone through struggles that only you know about. None of that matters now. Do you know why? It's because you have all the plays the other team is about to run. The title is yours already. All you have to do is stick to the game plan.

Choose Your Friends Wisely

In addition to looking out for players and the tactics they use to manipulate women, you should also pay close attention to the people you call your friends. Yeah, the girl you've been calling your best friend for a while now. I'm sure she knows more about you than anybody. Your friends may act as if they are happy for you, while jealously rages deep inside them. It might be a graduation, a wedding, a new home you recently purchased, or a promotion. A lot of women are happy for their friends up until the point when they feel they are suddenly doing better than them. Maybe you are engaged and one of your friends is still having problems finding a decent guy to hold a conversation with. You and your friends may have graduated high school together at the same time, but things may be unfolding for you a lot quicker. They may feel as if you are leaving them behind. Always pay attention to the little things they say.

For instance, your friend might feel like the guy you are dating is taking away the time you used to spend together as friends, going shopping, watching movies, etc. Pay close attention when and if your girlfriends start saying things like, "I don't like him," without any logical explanation or reasoning to back that statement up.

Your friend could secretly have a crush on your boyfriend or husband. All the animosity she expresses towards him could actually be masking the secret feelings she has for him that are slowly seeping out. I have been in many situations where the friend of a particular woman I'm talking to supposedly can't stand me. As soon as the woman I'm talking to leaves the room, her friend attempts to make eye contact with me.

In one case, the friend of a woman I was dating walked back and forth across the room trying to get my attention. You must know that some guys will fall for these tactics, and when they do you likely never find out about it. The reason you will probably never find out about them messing with your man is for the simple reason that your closest friends know your schedule the best. She will know about any opportunity to do something behind your back first because you tell her everything. Your best friend knows when you go to school, work, shopping, etc.

On top of that, a young player will try to get your friend to expose every secret she knows about you to him. He will attempt to use the same charms on her that he used on you. Your best friend has nothing to lose if she is already talking to him behind your back. This means the first thing she will do is start telling him every negative thing about you that she can think of and she may even make some things up.

This new breed of player could have your best friend thinking that he actually wants to be with her instead of you. She is willing to throw your entire friendship away for him. Most women have already told their friends how much of an awesome guy their man is all around. Don't you think that would have sparked her interest? Sometimes we welcome negative energy to our doorstep by bragging. That's why you shouldn't tell people everything about your business all the time. Your best friend could fall under the same spell of this player's lies and charm.

I will give an example of how to catch one of your friends if they are going behind your back. Let's say you have two best friends who may be a little too friendly with your boyfriend. Tell each friend something different regarding you talking to an ex, etc. Tell friend #1 that you saw your ex at the store and exchanged numbers. Tell her to make sure she doesn't tell a soul. Tell friend #2 that you met a new guy today at the mall and exchanged numbers. Tell her to make sure she doesn't tell a soul. Now let's say your boyfriend confronts you about you possibly cheating on him. It may be days later or even weeks. Regardless, if he mentions anything about an ex, you know friend #1 is the snake. If he mentions anything about giving your number to a guy at the mall then friend #2 is the snake. Your boyfriend has been exposed as well because he shouldn't be talking to your friends behind your back. A bad friend may even try to get you to talk to other guys so that she can sabotage your relationship with him on purpose. She will almost instantly run back and tell him in an attempt to break up your relationship. I advise you to keep your romantic relationship private, especially when it comes to your single girlfriends.

Hopefully you will never be in this situation. If you suspect that one of your close friends is snooping behind your back with your boyfriend or husband, but you're not sure which one, I will be the first to tell you to trust your instinct.

Let's imagine the scenario where your man has a second phone again, but the only difference now is the woman he's cheating with knows you. When this happens, it's almost impossible for you to prove anything is going on unless you catch him in the act. tIt's no longer one mind working against you, but two. The other woman, your so-called friend, is helping him because she wants your spot. She will use every trick she can think of to keep cheating with him.

They will go over their evil routine and schedules together carefully. I suggest you watch the woman you call your best friend first. Then you can keep an eye out on your co-workers, extended family, etc. It's never a bad idea to pop up somewhere early just to see what's going on while you were away.

I'm not saying that you can't trust anyone, but I do want to warn you that guys are becoming smarter and more careful and, in some cases, other women are helping them. If a woman is happy in her relationship and her friends are not, I bet more than half of her friends would be willing to go behind her back if they had the opportunity.

A lot of people care more about their own feelings than those of other people when it comes to jealousy and lust. In that small window of opportunity, trust me, huge damage can be done. I know it's a lot to think about and take in. However, arming yourself with this information can help to prevent such a betrayal from ever taking place.

And if you ever find yourself in the position of the best friend who becomes the other woman, think about it this way. In the mind of your best friend's guy, you are just another woman on a list of many that he talks to and can have sex with. There are no feelings or strings attached on his side. Remember, all he had to do was listen and agree with everything you said. Meanwhile the woman that he is currently in a relationship with or married to would never allow that which is why he respects her more. Do you see how easily heartbreak can put a woman in the very same position as the woman who came between her and her man in the first place?

Do not let your emotions put you in a position that blurs your vision for your life all because of a man who didn't deserve you in the first place. Although this is an experience that many women can testify to having been through, if you heed my warning, you can consider this one less situation you have to experience. Never give a man your time and definitely not your body if he has not found the power within himself to rise above temptation. Fidelity is something money cannot buy.

Strategies for Navigating Men

Now that I've taught you a few strategies and red flags to look out for, I'll arm you with some of your own strategies to uncover a man's true intentions. Think of it as your very own arsenal of secret weapons, equipped with the latest see-through goggles.

Keep a Lid on Your Emotions

Don't make mistakes based on your emotions. If possible don't even show any of your emotions besides laughter. Look at your emotions as if you were playing cards. Never show your hand.

You must control your feelings at all times. I believe no particular emotion is greater or more powerful than another. With that being said, if someone laughed for twenty-four hours nonstop, people would start to question their mental state, right? But if someone is upset for a few days, society views that as normal. That's almost insane to me. On top of that, stress and anxiety cause health risks. I view heartbreak, stress, and anything else that comes along with it as decoys that slow me down in life. And let me tell you, I won't be stopped. You won't be stopped. Taking control of your emotions gives you superhuman powers. You are able to stop potential arguments in a split second. You will become more focused because the negative things people may say about you will turn to faint whispers and before you know it you won't be able to hear them at all. When you become emotional, men who may have ulterior motives see your weaknesses. Stay focused and remember a guy's strategy is to make you feel comfortable around him. Once a guy has your attention, in his mind its game on.

One way to prevent a guy from playing games, strategies, and manipulation tactics is when you meet a new guy, don't mention anything about your previous relationships. Just tell him you on't want to talk about it, and he should respect that. Never give a man a choice but to respect you. You must demand respect at all times. If they don't respect you and act as if you don't exist. If they try to get your attention but won't call your name, then don't respond. Women can shape their own world. You don't want people around who are not abiding by your rules and your rules only show them the exit out of your life. A woman must stand on her word. Mean what you say and say what you mean. In order for a woman to demand respect, she must take control of whatever situation she finds herself in.

Make Him Do the Talking

Ask him questions and listen to what he has to say instead of doing most of the talking. If he is the one asking all the questions, he can easily manipulate the conversation because he is in the driver's seat. Imagine you are the only person on a deserted island that has billions of dollars of treasure hidden on it. If someone arrives on shore one day, would you simply answer all of their questions? No, of course not. You should immediately view them as a threat until you figure out their true intentions. Unless you ask the questions, you risk losing it all.

If you operate this way with men, you will more than likely exposed the type of guy he is up front. It's easier to catch someone in lies if you set traps for them to fall into. Your traps should be a series of questions or statements only that allow you to figure out his point of view and how he responds to different kinds of situations.

Tell him you are celibate, for instance, and ask him his opinion on celibacy. Ask if he has a lot of women as friends. Ask him if he's intimate with any of his friends. Ask why is he currently single. Ask him what his ex-girlfriends would say about him if you spoke to them. Ask him what legacy he plans on leaving in this world before he dies. Say to him, "What if I told you my father would kill and die for my respect and god only knows what he will do if you ever attempt to lay a hand on me." What will he say to that?

Pay Attention When His Lies Don't Add Up

Trust should be earned and not given away freely. A liar's worst enemy is someone with a good memory. Remember to question everything and eventually you will start noticing the things he says doesn't make any sense when he is lying. Once you catch him lying, how much more evidence do you need to leave him?

Time and time again we see women on talk shows who have spent thousands of dollars on private investigators to catch a guy cheating. They bypassed every red flag that told them he was no good from the start. Some women even go against themselves, ignoring their gut feelings. It's not worth the risk. If you see a stray dog outside foaming at the mouth and growling at you, what other red flags do you need to prevent you from going near it?

Men will judge you just as soon as they lay eyes upon you. They will try to read your body language and eye contact. They will also judge you based on the way you dress and how you respond to the questions they ask you. A guy can use the same line or question with every woman he meets. This is why you must take control of the conversation from the start without him knowing what's going on.

Remember, the easiest way to do this is by asking questions. Question everything. I cannot say that enough. Most women who fail to use this technique fall victim to game. The sweet nothings and captivating stories a man uses to woo a woman can be quite hypnotizing. These meaningless words might sound like sweet music to your ears. He might seem like he is the only good guy around if you become entangled in his webs. Soon, you'll be entranced and you won't know how to get out of his trap, similar a spider's prey.

Don't Be Fooled by Status, Money, or Fame

One way to avoid the allure of his material wealth and possessions is to make your own money. Then you will not be impressed by those things and you'll have no need to hang around those type of players. Stay focused on your personal goals and secure your education. This will ensure that you don't have to depend on a man financially. Because when you depend on a man financially, at some point he will try to control you.

I'm sure you don't have that problem, but if you do, please switch gears fast. Go home and live with your parents or relatives. Start over from scratch if you have to. Swallow your pride. Living at home and saving money is nothing to be ashamed of. Put yourself in a position where you can get ahead. The main focus should always be your own well-being and future first.

How to Catch a Cheater

One way to catch a serial cheater is by paying attention to which days he takes you out and where the dates take place. A player will not want to go out in the city where he is from or currently resides. The reason for this is he might already have a girlfriend or wife. I remember dating a woman who thought I lived with my mom. She believed this lie for years and never found out the truth.

Ask yourself a few questions. Why does he always ask to hang out in your city? Why do you only hang out at certain times of the week? Why do you only talk on the phone during the day and text at night? If you find yourself in this situation, don't settle for his excuses. Switch things up on him immediately. Stop following his routine. You are the Queen. You're the prize. He must prove to you why he deserves to be in your life and not the other way around. Try ignoring his calls and texts during the day. Call or video chat with him at night around 10 or 11 p.m.

Do this several times and remember to mix up the routine every few days. Never let him predict your next move because if he does, trust that he will be a step ahead of you again. If he doesn't answer you, that's a clear warning sign. And don't count on other women coming forward and confronting you about your boyfriend or husband. If he has potential, money, and a bright future, you can bet that other women will not care if he is currently in a relationship or not.

Some women only come forward when they feel a man has lost or withheld whatever he had been offering her. If he is not spending as much time with her, she will get mad as well. Whenever he is not with her, she is thinking about the time he is spending with you. I know it sounds crazy to think that some women will still pursue a man even when she knows he is in a relationship, but that is just how some women's minds operate.

Here's another important tip: avoid sending your man to the grocery store. It may seem harmless, but in reality, The opportunities for a man to meet other women behind your back in there are endless. I recommend making time to go the grocery store instead of sending your significant other. There are nearly four to five women in every aisle on a busy day. Sure, he got everything on the grocery list that you asked for, but what you don't know is there's probably a lot more that he forgot to mention to you.

Places like grocery stores or any heavily trafficked public places are easy targets for young players. A guy can easily spark up a conversation with a woman there by asking her about a specific product. Trust me, he is not concerned about the calories in a bag of chips and it's no coincidence he chose to ask her.

Do you want another strategy for figuring out if your current boyfriend or husband is a cheater? Never mind, I'm sure you are not interested. Smile, I'm only joking. On a serious note, before I give you yet another tip, I need you to ask yourself if you're ready for this information. I must warn you that the outcome to this setup could be overwhelming.

If you are still reading, I trust that you want proof and can handle the plan I'm about to explain to you. If every woman in a relationship tried this method, surely more than 50 percent of their significant others would fail. I strongly feel every woman should keep this strategy close by to verify their significant other's true identity early on before getting too attached to him or giving him something they can't take back.

Executing this plan should not take more than a month to reap results. Ask him to go to a particular grocery store or another place of your choosing a few times so that he can get comfortable in his new surroundings. Try to choose a place where there will be a lot of women, such as a mall, sporting event, or grocery store. Any of these locations will work, and they won't seem out of the ordinary.

Be aware that a man who thinks one step ahead will always be on high alert. He will always check the scene first and play it cool while observing the action surrounding him like a top-secret spy in a foreign country. Trust that he is checking out the scene for anyone who might recognize him and tie him back to you. If he sees anyone familiar, he will abort the mission. That is why it's important to let him go to the location a few times before you send in your mole. Now here comes the part that will blow your mind.

Ask a female friend from work, a relative, or any woman you trust that he will not recognize to help you by going to the super market as a decoy. Make sure it's someone who will not speak about this situation again, no matter the outcome. Think of a specific item to put on his grocery list and make sure you know exactly what aisle it's in. That way you can tell your partner in crime exactly where to find him when it's going down. Keep in mind you can use this same strategy at any store. Tell her to be in that specific aisle before he gets there. Ideally, you should put a lot of energy and brain power into this plan because the outcome is critical to the future of your relationship..

Don't forget to describe your significant other in precise detail, including the type of clothes he will be wearing. This way your friend can appear as an ordinary shopper and skip the aisles that he may be in until she meets up with him at the section of the store you specified. This is important because as I said earlier, young players observe everything. Go over everything you want her to say when she sees him ahead of time. This way you can find out and pin point his dirty ways. The best way for her to get his attention in a small place such as a grocery aisle is to wear some good perfume. That way when she walks by, his hound nose will get a good whiff of it. Not to mention the stunning outfit she should have on as well.

Remember, there is more than one way to cheat. Tell your accomplice not to be too aggressive. That will throw up a red flag and tip him off. I recommend she walk by and smile or create small talk. She can ask about a particular item in his shopping cart or whether he has ever tried a certain recipe. She could crack a small joke about how crowded the grocery store is or ask him if he knows where a certain item is located in the store. She could even ask him what school he attended because he looks so familiar. Either way, she needs to walk off and see if he follows or tries to meet up with her in the next aisle.

Ever wonder why he forgot some things on the list when you clearly wrote them down so that he wouldn't forget? It's possible he had his eye on a woman and lost track by trying to maneuver past the old lady and the child who's picking up items after his grandma told him to quit touching stuff in the store. Maybe he just wanted to get a glimpse of her outfit one more time.

If he does follow her, your accomplice needs to flirt with him a little. You are in control, so it can be short and sweet or you can tell her to follow him all the way out into the parking lot. It's your call. If he takes or asks for her number, what more proof do you need? He may not get her number, but if he tells her to meet him there again or at another location out of paranoia, then he's still committing the same sin.

Some women will say you should give him another chance even if he takes the bait or gets caught cheating because he will have learned his mistake. I say leave immediately because there's a 50/50 chance that he could look at you as a weak woman for believing the lies and games he's played since the day you met. The fact that it's a 50/50 chance is not worth it. Why would you gamble with your life and well-being that way? Your future is more important. Demand your respect.

Another strategy is to just buy a tape recorder like the small, yet powerful recorders detectives use. Leave it somewhere he spends a lot of time, like in his car under a seat. Maybe under the sofa or bed. Don't forget to turn it on when you leave the house. You may be surprised about what you find on the recorder so prepare yourself for the worst. You may not find anything on it. He may be a step ahead. That's why it's so important to me to get this message out to all the women around the world before it's too late. It's time to take a stand and demand respect from men.

Moving On with Your Life

Women often ask, "What's the best way to handle being cheated on?" My answer is time. The only way to get over it is to let time pass and your wounds heal. After a breakup, you should find something you enjoy doing to occupy your mind. Spend time with family and true friends. Take that time to shake the negative energy off and better yourself. Your ex was not the one, only a decoy to slow you down in life. It's his loss, not yours.

The last thing you should do is run to another guy for comfort. You will only help another player succeed at his foolery. You are worth far more than that.

Do not feel the need to post pictures on social media for likes or validation from others because you will eventually lose yourself in the process. Confidence is key; it will unlock a lot of doors for you while you're on this journey some call life.

I advise each and every woman to analyze any man who comes into her life very carefully. Ask yourself what makes him worthy of being in your presence. Time is valuable, and we can't afford to waste any of it.

Embracing Your Inner Queen

No more feeling intimidated or overpowered by boys dressed in men's clothing. No more feeling obligated to do anything for a man. Be free, be smart, be great at anything your heart desires. Do not waste your time with anyone who makes you feel anything less than a Queen. You are royalty. It's up to you to find your true power deep within yourself and the time is now.

Do not look for validation, power, courage, or confidence anywhere else because it all starts with you. Believing in yourself is a way of living. Now that you've read this book, you must implement my strategies into your day-to-day life. Don't be afraid of change. You will have better results in in the long run if you actually follow the steps and strategies I've outlined in my book.

Stay faithful to your beliefs as if they are religion. Read this out loud and with confidence:

> I do not need validation from anyone, especially not from a man. Everything in this world will try to convince me otherwise, from magazines to television. I am gold. I am powerful. I am magic. I will not be stopped. I will succeed.

Now, look around and you will see that almost every woman looks the same. A lot of women want the same clothes, the same makeup, and the same shoes. They are programmed that way so it's important for you to think for yourself. It's important that you are proud of your body, hair, skin tone, etc. Do not change anything about your physical features because some loser says you are not pretty.

Do not ever try to act a certain way or do certain things to fit in with a group. Never let anyone peer pressure you. That gut feeling you get when you sense something is not right—I suggest you listen to it. The more you cherish and protect yourself from any type of negativity, the closer you will get to the day when you will unleash the Queen you truly are. With any and every dream or goal you may have, it's important to make the proper steps towards that dream. You must keep a clear mind and remain focused. Your two biggest distractions in life will be yourself and a man. Rise above both. Challenge yourself to become a better woman every day. Seek knowledge, not attention. Use your time on this earth wisely. Nobody knows when it will be their time to go and the clock is ticking. There's no time to waste.

You will be attracted to some guys and that is normal. Now, what is not normal is allowing someone into your life based off looks alone. The most powerful and beautiful attribute you have is your mind. Don't let anyone take that from you.

To all the players out there, I hope this is the end for you. To every woman that's been hurt by one, I pray that this book marks a new beginning for you. With these last few words, I want to leave every woman with something to remember.

No matter how powerful or rich a man may appear to be, I want to assure you it's all an illusion. I don't care how successful he claims to be. I don't care how confident he may be at times. A real man knows the truth. Deep down we know who holds the real power. Yes, it's women. Every man that looks into his mother's eyes loses power instantly because he's overshadowed by love. Nothing else matters in that moment. If anybody thinks differently, I advise them to rethink their definition of a man.

If God is love, then woman is essentially God or at least the closest thing you can get to God in this earthly life. I pray that you become the Queen you are supposed to be. My gift to you is a key. It's time to unlock your magic and remember to love yourself, forever and beyond.